Night Animals

Claire Llewellyn

Night Animals

owl

bat

Night animals sleep in the day.
They come out at night.

Night animals hunt for food at night.

Owl

An owl hunts at night.
It hunts for mice and insects.

An owl has big eyes.
Its eyes help it to see in the dark.

Bat

A bat hunts at night.
It hunts for mice and insects.

A bat has big ears.

Its ears help it to hear animals move.

Raccoon

A raccoon hunts at night.
It hunts for fish and frogs.

A raccoon has long fingers.
Its fingers help it to feel under water.

Fox

This fox hunts at night.
It hunts for mice and birds.

This fox has big ears.
Its ears help it to hear animals move.

Kiwi

A kiwi hunts at night.
It hunts for insects.

A kiwi has a long beak.
Its beak helps it to smell under ground.

What Is It?

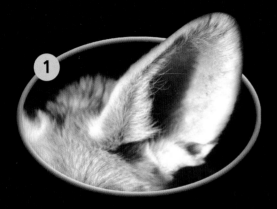

This night animal has big ears.

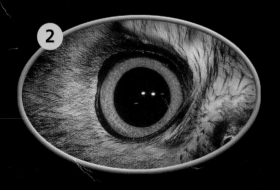

This night animal has big eyes.

Answers on page 16

This night animal
has long fingers.

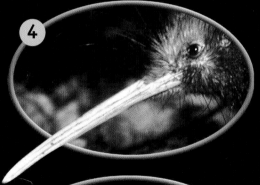

This night animal
has a long beak.

This night animal
has big ears.

Bat 6–7

Owl 4–5

Fox 10–11

Raccoon 8–9

Kiwi 12–13

Answers for pages 14–15: **1** fox, **2** owl, **3** raccoon, **4** kiwi, **5** bat